MEET Y CHAKRAS

BE YOUR BEST SELF

Chakra Healing Guide for Beginners

INDEX

YOUR SUBTLE BODY   7

FIRST CHAKRA: ROOT OR MULADHARA   23

SECOND CHAKRA: SACRAL OR SVADHISHTHANA   35

THIRD CHAKRA SOLAR PLEXUS OR MANIPURA   47

INTRODUCTION

I am so happy that you have decided to purchase this book, because I have written it with only one great purpose: to help you to keep your 7 chakras healthy so you can have emotional, mental, spiritual, and physical well-being.

You deserve the best; a full and satisfying life. You deserve the most intense experiences to enjoy every moment and develop your potential to the fullest, overcome your own limits and achieve your goals. You deserve to be happy, and if until now you have not been able to overcome some negative situation, experience, pain or emotion, or if you have not been able to move towards your ideal life reality, get ready to start a life free of obstacles.

What I am offering you are a series of chapters, easy to read, intended to help you in your personal growth by learning practices to open, activate, unblock and keep your chakras in balance.

If you don't know anything about this subject, don't worry about it. I have decided to develop this book with an easy to understand and practical language, in order to guide you in every step. And, if you already have knowledge on this subject, you will find on each page, a new light about the chakras. My intention is to help you to practice actions, attitudes and behaviors that maximize your well-being. I hope you enjoy reading, as much as I have enjoyed writing each page. And, at the end, we´ll find ourselves in the same place: freedom.

My best wishes,
Barbara

"You were born with wings, why prefer to crawl through life?"
- Rumi

Chapter 1
YOUR SUBTLE BODY

"As you start to walk on the way,
the way appears."
- Rumi

"There is nothing either good or bad but thinking makes it so."
- W. Shakespeare

MEET YOUR CHAKRAS

The most important human energetic structure of our entire body, as discovered by the Orientals more than 5,000 years ago, are these invisible and intact energy cores called Chakras. They have the ability to influence our own energetic harmony and the health of the entire body.

Multi-frequency energies flow through these centers, and they influence our mood, our emotions, and even the physiology of the heart itself.

Knowledge of the chakras and their relevance for vital energy is important because they reflect in the human body the way in which we process and administer both the daily information we receive, as well as thought and consciousness.

Throughout this book, we are going to go through the main 7 chakras; we are going to get to know them and understand what their role is within us. By understanding them, we can begin to take the first steps to heal them; in any case, you need it. This graph summarizes the functions of each of them and their location within our body.

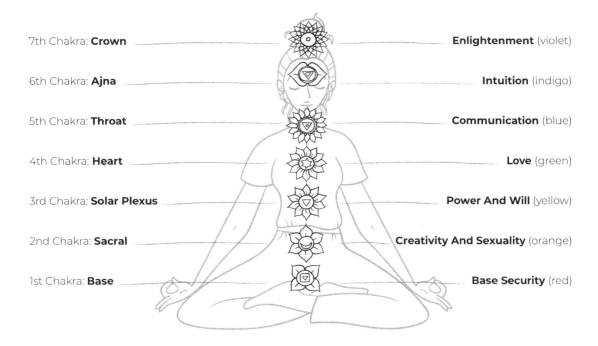

7th Chakra: **Crown** — **Enlightenment** (violet)

6th Chakra: **Ajna** — **Intuition** (indigo)

5th Chakra: **Throat** — **Communication** (blue)

4th Chakra: **Heart** — **Love** (green)

3rd Chakra: **Solar Plexus** — **Power And Will** (yellow)

2nd Chakra: **Sacral** — **Creativity And Sexuality** (orange)

1st Chakra: **Base** — **Base Security** (red)

DOES YOUR VITAL ENERGY FLOW?

Vital energy is in all living beings, without us being able to touch it or see it. It is intangible and invisible, but it vitalizes, as a specific immaterial force that differentiates living beings from inanimate ones.

When vital energy flows, a healthy effect is produced in oneself, which is transmitted when others feel our presence. On the other hand, when vital energy does not flow, the energy field of the people around us is negatively altered.

Keep in mind that energy flows smoothly in a healthy body, which is not nourished by worry, sadness, resentment, anger, or anxiety. In fact, when you get stuck with any of these feelings, you provoke an internal disorder. These are feelings of low vibration. And, the vital energy decreases, stagnates and does not flow freely. It is normal to feel them from time to time. The important thing is to know how and when to let them go and not get stuck in your desire to control them.

When you feel as though you're without enough strength to fully enjoy life, it means that your vital energy is not flowing.

Therefore, I can tell you that your vital energy flows when you enjoy good physical, mental, emotional, and spiritual health, and if you lack good health in one or more of these areas, it is necessary to activate your vital energy, to make it flow. This book is precisely about that - to help you activate your body's energy and make it flow freely.

You know that your energy flows when you feel good about yourself, when you feel good with those around you, when you feel satisfaction in life and live without fear. On the other hand, if you live in fear, dissatisfied, or if you are discouraged by obstacles, then your life energy is not flowing, and you need to take action.

Now, you can read the book to see how you can help yourself in every aspect of your subtle energy body, or you can also go directly to the chapter that talks about the topic you specifically want to address. Both options are perfect. I wish you a good journey!

THE PERSONAL POWER OF EACH CHAKRA

Each of the chakras is related to an important personal power that connects us with our intuition, with the internal wisdom that only comes from what we feel from the heart, and from the feelings.

AWAKENING YOUR ENERGY

It is possible to balance the vital energy so that it flows correctly and thus have well-being in all areas. Here, I will give you examples of things you should do to help boost your energy. As we advance in the chapters, you will see more detailed information according to each symptom that you may have. For now, I will advance you the topics that we will deal with in each chapter and give you a general overview for raising your energy:

- **Food:** Make sure you have a balanced diet. Without a good diet, energy levels drop. The more colors from nature you consume, the better. Mix fruits and vegetables so that your plate simulates a rainbow! This way, you will be activating the energies of all your chakras.

- **Meditation:** Meditation is essential to raise your vital energy. Silence your mind when it is noisy and enter a non-judgmental state that allows you to connect with your inner self. Feel your emotions without judging them. There are several studies that show the incredible benefits of meditation on our brain. My favorite is the one conducted by Sara Lazar from Harvard University, in which Lazar confirms that meditation is capable of changing brain structure for the better in people who practice it regularly. Among the benefits, the most important ones are: improves memory and learning, promotes creativity, improves sleep quality, lowers cortisol and blood sugar levels, reduces stress and anxiety; among many others. We will then see meditation exercises for each energy center.

- **Yoga or exercise:** It is necessary to practice exercises to channel your vital energy. Find a physical activity or sport that you are passionate about and do it for at least 30 minutes a day. My recommendation is that you try yoga since it will not only be an activity for your physical body, but also for your energetic body. There are yoga postures for each energy center and others to raise your vital energy. In the following pages, you will see the exercises.

- **Rest:** It is essential to have a good sleep and daily rest, so that your body and mind recover. At bedtime, you should disconnect your mind from work, pending activities and all worries. Educate yourself to sleep well and rest sufficiently.

- **Outdoor activities:** As the fifth point to balance your vital energy, it is important to connect with nature, through outdoor activities. Make that connection a habit. In each chapter, I will recommend activities related to each chakra so that you can channel its energy in the best way.

- **Quartz and stones:** Quartz are wonderful conductors and activators of energy. To activate your vital energy, have a crystal quartz nearby; this quartz is known as the ultimate healer. It is a healing stone with great power and pure energy that gives clarity to the mind.

- **Mantras:** Listen to and chant a mantra regularly. The energetic vibrations produced by mantras and their repetitive and rhythmic pronunciation have wonderful effects by slowing down the nervous system and calming the mind, which also brings incredible benefits to the cardiovascular system. The impact of mantras has an explanation that goes beyond the spiritual: Sound is a form of energy composed of vibrations or wavelengths. Certain vibrations have the power to heal while others can break a glass into small pieces. That is precisely the mantras, healing and calming sounds. As in the previous topics, there are mantras for each energy center. Read on to find out which one to use for each chakra.

- **Aromatherapy:** Just a few drops of the correct essential oil are enough, and your body's energy will begin to change. Aromatherapy is increasingly known for its effect on the alchemy of our physical and energetic body and even many clinics and hospitals currently use it as an alternative method to improve the recovery of patients. We used to underestimate the power of nature; however, with the correct combination of flowers and essences, you can "touch" your body to reduce anxiety, stress and calm you down.

- **Colors:** Like music, colors are capable of evoking emotions almost immediately, which in turn are reflected in physical responses. Colors have a profound effect on our subconscious and can alter our mood for better or for worse. Be careful with the colors you surround yourself with. If you have a preferred color, maybe in this book, you will understand which energy center it is linked to and you will be able to understand why you like to use it. The color white for example is a color that transmits peace and tranquility and therefore, it will help you lower levels of stress and anxiety.

- **Daily affirmations:** Affirmations can be a powerful tool to help you change your mood. The key here is to feel your affirmation as something that is already real, in each part of your body. You ought to feel the emotion that is behind each word and to stay in that feeling for as long as possible. With the correct affirmations, you can eliminate limiting beliefs, raise your energy and change your thinking process and make it work for you on your benefit. Here are some affirmations that you can repeat every day to raise your vital energy:

1. I am grateful for what I have.
2. I deserve the best and I accept it with open arms.
3. Today I am overflowing with energy.
4. Today I am better than yesterday.
5. I live in peace and harmony.

The best time of day to repeat daily affirmations is before bed and as soon as you wake up. It is in these states of tranquility that the subconscious is most receptive to receiving our instructions. As Wayne Dyer says, "You may have had a terrible day, but if 5 minutes before going to sleep, you find peace; your subconscious will take only that, peace."

- **Water:** Hydration is another factor that influences vital energy; remember that 75% of the body depends on water and our cells need the oxygen provided by water.

One of my favorite methods to raise my vibration amazingly fast is by consuming **solarized water or moon water**, and best of all, you can make it yourself!

Every time someone comes to my house, there are a thousand questions and comments. "What nice little bottles! What do you use them for? What do they have inside?" The answer is simple. I learned from Ho'ponopono that regular drinking water, if properly solarized, can immediately raise your vibrational frequency, protecting you and helping you heal from both physical and emotional illnesses.

On a spiritual level, solarized water erases painful memories, purifies your body of bad energies and helps you free yourself from what you don't need. You can drink it, use it for cooking, juices, bathe your whole body, use it as a tonic, wash your mouth, and water your plants, among others. When we drink this water, we are cleaning the toxic; this is explained by Dr. Hew Len, creator of the Ho'pono-pono technique. Considering that we are between 70 and 80% water, don't you think your body would like a daily dose of this vital energy that is available to everyone? For mine, it is spectacular!

All you must do is get blue glass bottles, fill them with drinking water (with a non-metal lid), leave them in the sun for at least 1 hour and voila, you have your energized water that your body will love! Besides making you feel spectacular, you will get sick a lot less (or almost never), isn't that great?

·   **Music:** Listen to relaxing music that transports you to some place of peace. Music has the power to change the energy of the environment where it is heard. There are waves of frequencies measured in Hertz (Hz) developed to activate different types of vibrational levels related to each chakra. In each chapter, we will see more details, although if you want to activate the vital energy of your whole body, I recommend the frequency of **432 Hz.**

The recommended frequencies for each energy center connect with the energy of each chakra and help to unblock trapped energies and release them. You can sleep with the frequency you consider appropriate and leave it on throughout the night, at a low volume so it doesn't get in the way of your sleep. While you sleep, you will unblock and clear energies that are trapped in your body. I recommend that you make this a daily habit so that you can feel its benefits.

Over the years, various studies have been developed in which it is established that music stimulates different areas of the body, promoting more brain activation than with any other stimulus. Some of the positive effects of music are:
·   Strengthens learning and memory.
·   Regulates hormones related to stress.
·   Modulates the speed of brain waves.
·   It regulates the heartbeat, blood pressure and pulse.

Good music strengthens the immune system and is reflected in a better health. For something, plants flourish more when there is background music and cows produce more milk with the right stimulus. The challenge is to find the notes that favor you in each specific situation.

My favorite study is one conducted by the Japanese Dr. Masaru Emoto. In which various drops of water are subjected to different stimuli, including different types of music, and Dr. Emoto publishes the results of how the structure of that drop of water changes just modifying the external stimulus. His studies are fascinating. As Dr Emoto says "Human thought, words, music, the labels on the containers, influence the water and it changes for the better absolutely. If the water does, we who are 70-80% water should behave the same."

It was after researching the results of Dr Emoto's studies that I began my studies in energy and learned to use it to my advantage. In this book, I summarize my preferred methods to keep my energy healthy and therefore, my physical body as well.

I wish you the best of experiences while reading this book. I have really enjoyed writing it with the aim of bringing a little bit of what I have learned in recent years to anyone who wants to raise their vibration and feel spectacular. I promise you one thing: by applying the advices that I give you here, you will never be the same again!

On the next page, you will find a summary of the actions that you must do to raise your vital energy.

RISE YOUR ENERGY AND ACTIVATE YOUR CHAKRAS

White

Affirmations (page 16)

Crystal quartz or moonstone

Frequency 432Hz

Yoga (page 21)

OM Mantra

Spend time in nature

Rainbow in your plate / solarized water

Meditation (page 20)

Essence of sandalwood or lavender

MEDITATION

TO RAISE YOUR VITAL ENERGY

I learned this technique from Joe Dispenza and it is one of my favorites. It is a breath in which I feel that I "undo the pipes" of the chakras and unlock vital energy to flow freely. After doing it, I feel more energized than if I just had 3 cups of coffee.

- Inhale deeply while contracting the internal muscles of the perineum as you inhale.
- While inhaling, shrink the muscles of the lower abdomen and then those of the upper as if trying to push the energy upwards.
- Maintain tension in these areas for a few seconds and continue inhaling a little more.
- Contract your chest and focus on bringing the energy from the base of your body to the crown of your head.
- When your attention reaches the crown, it will be time to hold your breath; continue squeezing and squeezing the energy upwards.
- Feel on the tip of your crown as if a fireworks party were exploding; hold the air as long as you can while contracting.
- Exhale deeply and breathe at your own pace for 1 minute and repeat the exercise 4-5 more times.

TO ENERGYZE YOUR BODY AND CONNECT WITH YOURSELF

- Sit comfortably, with your spine erect and with your eyes closed, breathe deeply.
- Inhale gently for a 7 count to energize each cell of your body; feel how the air from your inhalation reaches every corner in your body.
- Hold your breath for a 7 count to help your body regulate itself.
- Exhale for a count of 7 and expel away everything that does not serve you.
- Hold your breath for a count of 7.
- Repeat this process 7 times.

YOGA ASANAS TO RAISE YOUR VITAL ENERGY

These are some postures that you can practice to raise your vital energy. Stay in each posture for 3-4 minutes and breathe deeply as you practice them.

VIRABHADRASANA I
WARRIOR POSE I

VIRABHADRASANA II
WARRIOR POSE II

DHANURASANA
BOW POSE

PURVOTTANASANA
UPWARD PLANK POSE

Chapter 2
FIRST CHAKRA:
ROOT or MULADHARA

SECURITY AND INSTINCT. KNOW YOUR ROOTS!

In this chapter, I want to introduce you to all the information you need to know about the first chakra. With this approach, you will be able to understand what the root chakra or Muladhara is, why it is blocked, and so much more. So read very carefully and enjoy the knowledge.

UNDERSTAND THE MULADHARA TO ACTIVATE ITS POWER

The root chakra, or Muladhara is the energy center that manages and controls the primary impulses that govern our life. It is the most physical chakra and the one of fundamental support; if you were a tree, this chakra would be the roots, hence its name. The first chakra connects us and gives us strength in our life. It is our connection to our inherited beliefs that gives us the feeling of belonging to a tribe, to feel welcome at our core.

The energy of the first chakra begun to vibrate since you were in the womb. From that moment, you felt the connection with your family nucleus and if you will be welcomed. From the moment you were born, connections and ties with family beliefs begun to be forged.

- · It is connected to the feeling of security and the ability to provide the basic self-preservation needs of life: food, sleep, and shelter.
- · Physical security in the family or group. Feel comfortable at home.
- · Ability to assert yourself and defend yourself.

This Chakra is located at the end of the spine, between the anus and the sexual organs; it is related to the organs of elimination, with the legs, bones and feet.

When the root chakra is blocked, fear, instability, and greed reign in your life. The main fear is of not surviving physically or of being left by the group - by the tribe. Through interactions with family and other groups in the early years of life, you learn how painful it can be to become excluded from a group and its protective energy. Therefore, when you grow up, you have that feeling of wanting to belong to a group at any cost.

On the other hand, when the root chakra works perfectly, and integrates well with the other chakras, you become a confident, stable, loyal, firm, and self-determined person. You develop resilience and a keen sense of belonging to yourself. There is a feeling of having solids roots, and you do not suffer from emotional lack or feeling adrift, the bases for automatic self-confidence are activated in you.

WHY IS THIS CHAKRA BLOCKED?

The base chakra or root chakra is blocked mainly when you do not feel that your roots in life are solid. When there is a feeling of not belonging or not being accepted in your family nucleus. When you feel that you are not welcomed. It is also blocked by fear, when you allow fear to affect you, and you cannot transmute or conquer it.

This chakra is also blocked when you seek power and security through money, or when you allow yourself to be burdened by responsibilities and lose your inner center.

Staying stuck in attitudes such as anger, aggressiveness, rage, excessive competition, and distrust, among others, blocks the base or root chakra, and condemns you to live without balance.

So, it is convenient for you to learn to identify when this chakra is blocked, when it is open and how you can balance it to recover the physical, mental, emotional, and spiritual well-being that it provides you.

CHECKING YOUR CHAKRA

There are symptoms that allow us to identify when the root chakra is blocked; you can feel restless, as if you were searching for something that you do not know what it is.

Also, when it is difficult for someone to settle down, it is a symptom of a blocked Muladhara chakra.

If you have any of the following symptoms listed below, you may have a blocked first chakra. Here is a fun exercise for you to know how to identify your root chakra. Mark the thermometer; for each symptom, color a level.

- Extreme restlessness.
- Feeling of Instability.
- Anger and aggressiveness.
- Continual impatience.
- Greed.
- Obsession for material things.

There are also physical symptoms or discomforts, and they are:

- Constipation.
- Low back pain.
- Eating disorders.
- Kidney stones.
- Weakness in the legs.

Barely living. Resurrection cart!

Struggling, hands on

Sort of surviving

Ok but some work needed

Thriving, ready for next level!

NOW START HEALING
YOUR ROOT CHAKRA

I AM. HEAL YOUR ROOT CHAKRA!

- **Surround yourself with red:** The vibration of red helps to balance the root chakra, so it is important to know how to use it: wear red underwear, eat red food, such as bell peppers, tomatoes, and chili peppers; use visual aids with vibrant red tones.
- **Stones:** Fire agate, tiger eye, ruby or tourmaline will activate the energy of your root chakra. Wear them on necklaces or just place them on your nightstand to feel their energy.
- **Yoga:** Do the recommended yoga asanas daily to activate the energy of this chakra detailed on page 31.
- **Outdoor activities:** All activities that involve leg strength are wonderful for the root chakra, and even better if you are barefoot as you will connect with the energy of the earth. So, walk barefoot, jump barefoot or just run. This will move the energy out of your root chakra and remove blockages.
- **Aromatherapy:** Cloves, cedar, citronella or patchouli. These essences vibrate with the energy of the first chakra.
- **Meditation:** Do the root chakra meditation on page 30 daily to activate its energy.
- **Food:** Eat foods that come out of the ground, preferably red: vegetables, roots, and tubers. Proteins, grains, and cereals.
- **Mantras:** Listen and repeat daily the mantra LAM (laaaaaammm)
- **Music:** Listen to the Frequency 396 Hz and leave it on.
- **Daily affirmations:** Repeat the following affirmations every day when you wake up and before going to bed:

1. My life flows in abundance.
2. I am safe and secure.
3. I am where I need to be.
4. I am enough.

I AM. HEAL YOUR ROOT CHAKRA!

Red

Affirmations (page 28)

Fire agate, tiger's eye or tourmaline

Frequency 396Hz

Asanas (page 31)

Mantra LAM

Walk barefoot and move your legs

Food from the ground, grains, and cereals

Meditation (page 30)

Essence of cedar, citronella, or patchouli

ROOT CHAKRA MEDITATION

Do this meditation every day to balance your base chakra energy:

- Sit in a comfortable position, preferably on the ground in contact with the earth / nature. Close your eyes.
- Visualize how tiny roots come out of your thighs that go deep into the earth and are charged with vital energy. The roots are bright and full of light.
- With each breath, every time you inhale, you are going to bring this vital energy to your body, and you are going to charge yourself with it.
- You are filled with light from the earth that goes directly to your root chakra and recharges.
- Exhale freely while the energy expands through your body.
- Feel how your root chakra glows with an incandescent red light.

Repeat the grounding breath for 3-5 minutes every day.

ROOT CHAKRA

YOGA ASANAS

These are some postures that you can practice to open and energize your root chakra. Stay in each posture for 3-4 minutes and breathe deeply.

MALASANA
GARLAND POSE

UTKATASANA
CHAIR POSE

VRKSASNA
TREE POSE

SUKHASANA
EASY POSE

OUTDOOR ACTIVITIES

The element of the root chakra is the earth; that is why the best exercises to activate its energy are those that are practiced barefoot as you intensify your connection. Color this element and feel how you connect with your roots.

emotions · creativity · sexuality · feelings · pleasure

—— Chapter 3 ——
SECOND CHAKRA:
SACRAL OR SVADHISHTHANA

CREATIVITY AND EMOTION. KNOW YOUR FLOW!

I congratulate you for reaching this third chapter, where I am going to introduce you to the second chakra, known as the sacral chakra or Svadhistana; its color being orange.

UNDERSTAND THE SVADHISTANA TO ACTIVATE ITS ENERGY

The sacral chakra or Svadhistana is the second energy center, and is related to the water element. It influences creativity, feelings and desire. It is related to our ability to flow with life, to enjoy it, and to let go of control, just as water flows regardless of the container in which it is.

It is located in the lower abdomen, just below the navel and is related to the reproductive glands, the kidneys and the bladder.

This is the chakra of relationships and its energy has vibrated since you were approximately 7 years old, since it is the age when children begin to interact with other children and begin to experience the world from a perspective outside the usual safety of their family nucleus. They begin to individualize and become more independent, to experience their ability to enjoy life and to flow. The energy moves from following the tribe to beginning to meet each as a separate individual and to discover other satisfying relationships.

The main challenge of the second chakra lies in the power of choice that we all have. Normally, we constantly search for the perfect choice for any crossroads (car, partner, clothes, friends, etc.), making ourselves believe that we are in control by "dominating" the outcome of that situation. This gives us a false sense of control and security fueled by fear. The need to want to control the results is nothing more than a manifestation of insecurity.

The characteristics of the second chakra are:
- Allows recognition and awareness of one's own feelings.
- A person who has the second chakra open does not move due to external pressure, he knows how to consciously relate to others and chooses unions with people that add to his growth and releases the people who impede it.
- The energy of the sacral chakra is very unstable because it wants to create, it wants to flow and be carried away by the desire and enjoyment of life. Creative energy constantly challenges the need for control in our lives.
- Sex is presented as a search for self-expression, a way to express the satisfaction that comes from relating to the outside world.
- Establishes a perfect combination of creativity, passion and charisma.

When you have this chakra in balance, your emotions flow freely and you can establish harmonious relationships with others. It allows you to develop your ability to generate ideas and put creativity into action and develop it to the fullest. You can also give and receive physical and sexual pleasure without problems.

WHY IS THIS CHAKRA BLOCKED?

The reasons why the Sacral Chakra can be blocked are related to unfavorable experiences that we had in our first years of life, around 6-10 years, when we began to socialize outside our family nucleus and our tribe. The basic feeling that blocks the sacral chakra is the feeling of guilt; when you are disappointed in your way of proceeding. If you feel guilty, that negative energy is absorbed by the chakra and it is blocked. The energy stagnates and this feeling of guilt does not let you move forward.

Now, there are other situations that block the sacral chakra; these are:
- Being in constant contact with toxic relationships in which you feel that you cannot express your creativity or flow with your natural instincts.
- Inability to flow with life and wanting to control every outcome.
- Feel remorse or regret in any way you act or think.
- Sexual abuse or rape.
- When in your family circle (tribe), sex is a taboo.
- Consumption of drugs or toxic substances.

It also blocks when you have a negative emotional situation with a family member or friend. Which is because, emotionally speaking, this chakra is related to contact and relationships in general.

CHECKING YOUR CHAKRA

Pay attention to symptoms on a physical level and symptoms on an emotional level. If you have any of the following symptoms listed below, you may have a blocked second chakra. Mark the thermometer; for each symptom, color a level.

As for the physical symptoms, they are:
· Impotence, frigidity or lack of libido.
· Lower back and pelvic pain.
· Problems with the reproductive system.
· Urinary problems.
· Lower back pain and sciatica.

The emotional symptoms are:
· Accusation and guilt.
· Stiffness and fear of enjoyment.
· Isolation.
· Need to establish power over others.
· Lack of creativity.
· Need to establish control in various aspects of your life.
· Lack of ethics in relationships.

Barely living. Resurrection cart!

Struggling, hands on

Sort of surviving

Ok but some work needed

Thriving, ready for next level!

NOW START HEALING YOUR **SACRAL CHAKRA**

Life can be amazing

**Live it,
love it,
enjoy it**

+Let go!

I FEEL. HEAL YOUR SACRAL CHAKRA!

Are you ready to establish the perfect balance of your second chakra?

- **Surround yourself with orange:** The energy of orange helps move the energy of the second chakra. Dress in orange, paint a wall in your room in this color or place pictures that have this color.
- **Stones:** Carnelian, orange aventurine, amber or citrine will activate the energy of your sacral chakra. Wear them as you prefer!
- **Yoga:** Do the recommended yoga asanas daily to activate the energy of this chakra detailed on page 43.
- **Outdoor activities:** Go swimming! Preferably in nature (sea, river, and lagoon) and feel the freedom of water, as its nature is precisely to flow with life. Another amazingly effective way to balance the sacral chakra is dancing. Fluid rhythms, such as salsa, cumbia, and partner dances, activate the second chakra. Use music that awakens joy that brings out your emotions.
- **Aromatherapy:** Essence of orange, cinnamon, sandalwood, patchouli or jasmine.
- **Meditation:** Do the sacral chakra meditation on page 42 daily to activate its energy.
- **Food:** Eat antioxidants rich foods, blue fish that contain omega 3.
- **Mantras:** Listen and repeat the mantra VAM (vaaaaam) daily.
- **Music:** Listen to the 417 Hz Frequency and leave it on.
- **Daily affirmations:** Repeat the following affirmations every day when you wake up and before going to bed:
1. I express my creativity freely.
2. I open my sensitivity to enjoy life.
3. I enjoy my life and my sexuality.
4. I am in balance and flow with life.
5. I love and take care of my body.

I FEEL. HEAL YOUR SACRAL CHAKRA!

Orange

Affirmations (page 40)

Carnelian, orange aventurine or amber.

Frequency 417Hz

Asanas (page 43)

Mantra VAM

Swim or dance

Antioxidant vegetables, omega 3

Meditation (page 42)

Essence of orange, cinnamon, sandalwood, patchouli or jasmine

CAT-COW BREATH TO ACTIVATE YOUR SACRAL ENERGY

- Position yourself comfortably at 4 points, preferably on the ground in contact with the earth / nature. Close your eyes, and take a deep breath.
- Inhale and bend your spine to the cow posture, stay 3-4 seconds and exhale and bring your spine to the cat posture and stay there for 3-4 seconds.
- Repeat this cat-cow breath for 3 minutes.
- Sit cross-legged and let the released energy settle in you and your body for another 1-2 minutes.

INHALE

EXHALE

SACRAL CHAKRA

YOGA ASANAS

These are some postures that you can practice to open and energize your sacral chakra. Stay in each pose for 3-4 minutes and breathe deeply.

KSEPANA MUDRA POSE

JANU SIRSASANA
HEAD ON KNEE POSE

BADDHA KONASANA
BUTTERFLY POSE

MUKHA SVANASANA
UPWARD FACING DOG POSE

OUTDOOR ACTIVITIES

The element of the sacral chakra is **WATER**. It brings great teachings to our life: The main one is that water always flows, like a river, which does not doubt its course or its direction; it simply surrenders to its flow to advance to end up joining with the ocean. My favorite activity to activate the sacral chakra is to go swimming and feel like I surrender to the fluidity of the nature of the water.

Chapter 4
THIRD CHAKRA
SOLAR PLEXUS or MANIPURA

PERSONAL POWER. KNOW YOUR INNER STRENGTH!

I welcome you to the fourth chapter of the book. I am excited to know that you continue to advance. I hope you put into practice the different ways of balancing the different chakras that I have been presenting to you so far.

It is time to talk about the third chakra, and I hope this information is of great benefit to you. It is about the solar plexus or Manipura; it is related to your personal power, vitality, and your personal energy. It is with this chakra that you strengthen your self-esteem and define the way you relate to yourself to interact with the outside. Unlike the first or second chakra whose energy invites you to relate to others, the third chakra is only yours and vibrates with your personal power in relation to the external world. For example, with your work, your hobbies and any activity that is yours, but involves the outside world.

UNDERSTAND THE MANIPURA TO ACTIVATE ITS ENERGY

The third chakra is also known as the solar plexus; in Sanskrit it is called Manipura and is located two fingers above the navel, in the upper part of the stomach.

Among its characteristics, the following can be mentioned:
- Its element is fire, and it is associated with the sun, its archetype being the warrior or the worker.
- Its color is yellow or deep gold.
- It governs the way you approach the world and how you relate to yourself in the outside world.
- Echoes the emotional energy and personality center.
- With the energy of the third chakra, you reach emotional maturity.

Being a chakra that relates your inner power together with your external connection, according to my point of view, it is one of the main chakras, since the way one feels about oneself will determine the quality of your life and your experiences. When you have a balanced Manipura chakra, you can experience the feeling that your life depends on yourself. You become a person of action, who can direct and develop your reality according to your personal interests. It is a chakra with which you can project your life, define a vision, and fulfill your mission, act in coherence with your well-being and with what you want to achieve.

If you do not have a balanced with Manipura chakra, you may have many good ideas, and incredibly good intentions, but you will not be able to put them into practice since you lack that innate energy of personal power, vitality and strength to carry out and accomplish your goals.

WHY IS THIS CHAKRA BLOCKED?

Nobody is born with good or bad self-esteem; this is something that is learned over the years with your interactions with the external world. As you face challenges from birth, you test your ability to decide who and what has power, and you learn how to obtain it and to use it. If you are in a healthy environment and achieve internal vitality, then your self-esteem is strengthened and you have a healthy solar plexus chakra; but if you decide that you do not have it or that you are not able to obtain it, you begin to live in a "power debt" in which at all times, you look for external sources of power that validate what you cannot do for yourself. You constantly seek approval or external reinforcement to feel good about yourself. The challenge we all have is to get enough inner strength not to depend on "external food" for power.

When situations in life cause you to lower your esteem or self-respect and you are not able to find it again within yourself, your solar plexus blocks its energy. Our ability to find this power within us also lies in how well we form the foundations with the previous chakras: the first and second chakras. Like everything in life, a good foundation helps the construction of any building to be more solid and resistant against any storm.

If you place your source of power outside, you empower others to erode your will and quench your life purpose. It is as if you are a horse and give the reins of your life to anyone who wants to take them.

Another manifestation of a weak or blocked third chakra is when due to your own lack of self-confidence, you become a manipulative person and try to control your friends and family to achieve a false sense of control over external things, since internally, you feel that you do not have the right control of your life. To heal, you first need to believe in yourself. That is why the energies that are within this chakra have a main objective, which is to help us in our own understanding, in the relationship with ourselves and the way in which we hold ourselves; because if you don't understand yourself and embrace your lack of self-esteem first, you can't begin to heal. Being honest with yourself is the first step.

When your solar plexus chakra is open, it manifests with behaviors and sensations such as:

- Sociable and open personality, feeling more curiosity in life and motivation to be better every day.
- Balanced emotions.
- Correct behavior of the organs that clean toxins.

CHECKING YOUR CHAKRA

Like the previous chakras, a blocked solar plexus is identified by several symptoms. Follow this exercise and mark the thermometer; for each symptom, mark or color a level.

The physical symptoms are:
· Irregular metabolism, stomach problems, or stomach ulcers.
· Problems in the central part of the spine, pancreas, or liver.
· Eating disorders.
· Diabetes and hypertension.
· Permanent fatigue.
· Skin problems.

Emotional symptoms include the following:
· Lack of personal power, insecurity, and self-esteem.
· Constant victimization.
· Anger and irritability.
· Procrastination.
· Stress and resentment.
· Lack of life goals and fear of not fulfilling responsibilities.
· Hypersensitivity to criticism.
· Megalomania.
· Lack of capacity to generate action and handle a crisis; there is compulsive doubt.

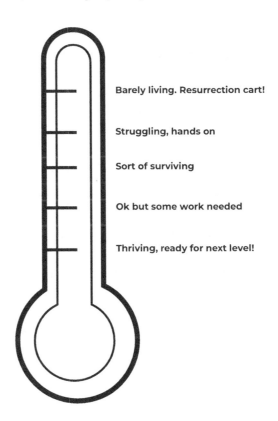

Barely living. Resurrection cart!

Struggling, hands on

Sort of surviving

Ok but some work needed

Thriving, ready for next level!

I DO. HEAL YOUR SOLAR PLEXUS!

Quoting the words of Polonius in the play, Hamlet, by W. Shakespeare, we begin this section: "Be true to yourself, because without personal power, life can be a terrible and painful experience."

- **Surround yourself with yellow:** This color helps you to work on your identity, perseverance, and your willpower; it influences you so that you can complete any project you have in mind. You can dress in yellow, surround yourself with yellow decorative elements in your home or office, or you can paint this color on the wall. Having a yellow card at your fingertips helps you in times of crisis: just breathe looking at that card for a few seconds and find calm. Concentrating for at least 5 minutes on the yellow color, while regulating your breathing is a way to keep the third chakra active.
- **Quartz:** The stones that activate this chakra are yellow jade, citrine, tiger's eye or yellow calcite.
- **Yoga:** Do the recommended yoga asanas daily to activate the energy of this chakra detailed on page 57.
- **Outdoor activities:** Sunbathe! This is my favorite activity to activate this chakra. Just don't forget to take care of your skin. You can also watch the sunrise or sunset. Any activity that involves the sun will be wonderful to activate this third chakra. Lie under the sun and visualize how your solar plexus connects with it and how it recharges with this wonderful energy.
- **Aromatherapy:** Smell essence of ylang-ylang, bergamot or lemon.
- **Meditation:** Do the solar plexus meditation on page 56 daily and activate your personal power.
- **Food:** Eat yellow foods such as: ginger, honey, corn, lemon or pineapple.
- **Mantras:** Listen and repeat daily the mantra RAM (raaaaam)
- **Music:** Listen to the 528 Hz Frequency and leave it on
- **Daily affirmations:** Repeat the following affirmations every day when you wake up and before going to bed.
1. I accept and value myself as I am.
2. My personal power is stronger every day.
3. I am safe and at peace.

*"Yesterday I was clever, so I wanted to change the world,
today I am wise, so I am changing myself."
-Rumi*

I DO. HEAL YOUR SOLAR PLEXUS!

Yellow

Affirmations (page 52)

Yellow Jade, Citrine or Yellow Calcite

Frequency 528Hz

Asanas (page 57)

Mantra RAM

Sunbathe or watch the sunrise and sunset!

Yellow food such as corn, lemon, pineapple

Meditation (page 56)

Ylang-ylang, bergamot or lemon essences

SOLAR PLEXUS MEDITATION

Do this meditation every day to balance the energy of your solar plexus chakra.

- Sit in a comfortable position. Close your eyes.
- Put your fists on your thighs doing the fire mudra according to the figure on this page.
- With each breath, draw the air through your nostrils, into your throat and lungs. Observe how it flows slowly and how it reaches your solar plexus.
- Visualize your solar plexus in the area between your ribs as if it had an incandescent light.
- Each time you inhale, you fill with light that goes directly to your solar plexus, and with each exhalation, pronounce the mantra RAM (raaaaaaammmm).

Repeat the solar breath for 3-5 minutes every day.

FIRE MUDRA

SOLAR PLEXUS CHAKRA

YOGA ASANAS

Here are some poses that you can practice to open and energize your solar plexus chakra. Stay in each pose for 3-4 minutes and breathe deeply.

VAKRASANA
HALF SPINAL TWIST POSTURE

TRIKONOSANA
TRIANGLE POSE

VIRABHADRASANA I
WARRIOR POSE I

VIRABHADRASANA III
WARRIOR POSE III

OUTDOOR ACTIVITIES

Connecting with our inner flame, the one which gives you power, is the first step to activate the solar plexus chakra. There is nothing more powerful than the sun itself and its extraordinary nature made with fire. With any activity that involves being in the presence of the sun, you will be empowering your solar plexus chakra.

Chapter 5

FOURTH CHAKRA:

HEART OR ANAHATA

UNCONDITIONAL LOVE AND GRATITUDE: KNOW YOUR INNER WORLD!

Now we come to the fourth chakra, which represents a vital energy center, which is why I ask you to pay close attention to this information and put it into practice to maintain your well-being and enjoy a healthy balance at all levels.

While the third chakra focuses on feelings towards us to face the outside world, this fourth chakra vibrates with emotions towards our inner world; our emotions towards our thoughts, ideas, and inspirations. The energy of the fourth chakra is pure power. Unconditional love has the power to heal us, lift us up, and inspire us.

The deep emotions that we may feel, whether of love or of past hurts, are related to the heart chakra, and listening to them is the first step in healing our inner child. If you decide to numb them with travel, shopping, or with any material way, contact with your emotions is obstructed, thus postponing an inevitable pain, and remaining anchored in the past. Remember that the material forms are linked to the first 3 lower chakras. Nobody says that it is not pleasant to go on a luxurious vacation, but with this, you will only be connecting with the third chakra. To connect with the energy of the fourth chakra, it is necessary to go within yourself to connect with your "inner self" and listen to its concerns, aspirations, motivations, and thoughts. Knowing your "inner person" activates your transformation.

Loving yourself unconditionally is related to freeing yourself from the domain of the "wounded inner child" with which you normally live. It means loving yourself enough to break the chains of the past and forgive the people who hurt you. Forgiveness is not an option if you want to truly heal; it is a requirement for your liberation. You move from the energies of the first 3 chakras that are based on connections with the outer world to focus on your inner world. We have analyzed the first chakra that focuses on the needs of the family and the tribe, the second chakra that connects with the first ties of friendship or relationship outside the tribe and those of the third chakra that vibrate in relation to our energy to face the external world. Now with the heart chakra, we solely focus on ourselves, on connecting with our inner world and on knowing and loving ourselves, unconditionally.

UNDERSTAND THE MANIPURA TO ACTIVATE ITS ENERGY

Its symbol is a six-pointed star formed by two triangles, one of the triangles points upwards and the other downwards, which represents a point of balance in the body between the flow of energy that goes towards the sky and towards the earth. That is why its element is air, which is the element that unites heaven and earth, the element that unites our earthly world with the highest.

The fourth chakra, which is located right in the center of our energetic body, connects the earthly chakras, which are the first three that we already analyzed (Root, Sacral and Solar Plexus) with the three superior ones that we will analyze in the following chapters (Throat, Third Eye and Crown).

In summary, the heart chakra is characterized by enabling us the ability to:
- Identify the sense of one's own limits, to delimit our internal world and differentiate it from the exterior or material world.
- Know who you are and connect with our inner self.
- Its element is air that connects the material world with the sky.
- Its color is: Intense green.

WHY IS THIS CHAKRA BLOCKED?

When you feel some deep pain or some negative emotion, and instead of allowing yourself to experience the feeling and letting it flow, going through it and living its shadows and darkness; you try to stop it with distractions coming from the material world, that is when your heart chakra is affected. Our goal is to love ourselves even when all we see is darkness. When you fail to love yourself unconditionally, or when you cannot put yourself first and instead, you prioritize the interests of the group, you are seriously affecting the vibration of the fourth chakra. When you stay on the substitute list of your own life, you are blocking your own energy.

CHECKING YOUR CHAKRA

When the heart chakra is open, it can be identified because you experience unconditional love for yourself, above all, wholeness, and compassion. It can also be identified because you enjoy life regardless of the outside world and feel a deep sense of gratitude for your life as it is.

To know if you have a blocked heart chakra, it is necessary to go to its symptoms. Mark the thermometer; for each symptom, color a level.

The emotional manifestations are:
- Excessive fear of loneliness.
- Being afraid of falling in love or being constantly jealous.
- Avoid having contact with others.
- Resentment, persecution of painful memories and inability to forgive others.
- General distrust of life and of others.

The physical manifestations are:
- Heart diseases.
- Problems with the immune system / Thymus.
- Problems in the circulatory system.
- Respiratory problems (e.g., asthma, allergy, pneumonia).
- Rib, breast problems (e.g., breast cancer).
- Problems in the neck, arms, or hands.

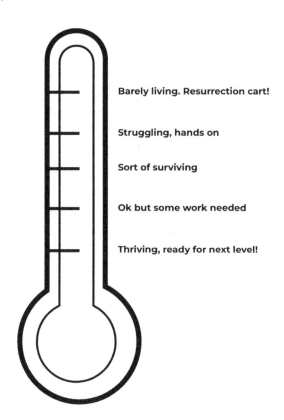

Barely living. Resurrection cart!

Struggling, hands on

Sort of surviving

Ok but some work needed

Thriving, ready for next level!

NOW START HEALING YOUR **HEART CHAKRA**

I LOVE. HEAL YOUR HEART!

- **Surround yourself with green:** Green is the color of this chakra. I recommend a walk in the countryside, appreciate the green of nature, bathe in its richness and feel the healing energy within you. You can also use green in clothing or decorating your home.
- **Stones:** Rose quartz, tourmaline or green jade will activate the energy of your heart chakra. Let your creativity fly in how to use them, but always have them with you.
- **Yoga:** Do the recommended yoga asanas daily to activate the energy of this chakra detailed on page 69.
- **Outdoor activities:** Walk through nature with open arms, feeling your heart completely open and full of love. Feel the fresh air on your face and connect your outer physical world with your inner world, which only you have access to. Feel the freedom that comes with that emotion. Contemplate the beauty of the flowers, look up and notice the color of the sky and the clouds; let yourself be enveloped in these natural wonders.
- **Aromatherapy:** Smell essence of lavender or rose.
- **Meditation:** Do the heart chakra meditation on page 68 daily and connect with your inner world.
- **Food:** Green food such as apple, kale, spinach, lettuce, and broccoli.
- **Mantras:** Listen and repeat the YAM mantra (yaaaaammm) daily.
- **Music:** Listen to Frequency 639 Hz and leave it on.
- **Daily affirmations:** Repeat the following affirmations every day when you wake up and before going to bed:

1. I am the most important thing in my life.
2. I love myself.
3. I am love.
4. I shine with my own light.

I LOVE. HEAL YOUR HEART!

Green

Rose quartz, tourmaline or green jade

Affirmations (page 66)

Asanas (page 69)

Frequency 639Hz

Walk outdoors and feel the wind on your face

Mantra YAM

Green foods: spinach, lettuce and broccoli

Meditation (page 68)

Lavender or rose

ANAHATA MEDITATION

Do this meditation every day to balance the energy of your heart chakra.

- Sit in a comfortable position. Close your eyes.
- Take 3 deep breaths.
- With each inhalation, open your arms as if you were a bird flying high. Feel how your heart fills with love, and share this love with the universe. Open your arms as wide as you can, pushing your chest forward.
- With each exhalation, close your arms and bring all the love of the universe towards you; your heart will grow stronger. With each exhalation, repeat the mantra YAM (yaaaaammmmm).
- Repeat heart breathing for 3-5 minutes every day.

INHALE

EXHALE

HEART CHAKRA

YOGA ASANAS

These are some postures that you can practice to open and energize your heart chakra. Stay in each pose for 3-4 minutes and breathe deeply.

USTRASANA
CAMEL POSE

BHUJANGASANA
COBRA POSE

SETU BANDHA SARVANGASANA
BRIDGE POSE

PURVOTTANASANA
UPWARD PLANK POSE

OUTDOOR ACTIVITIES

AIR is the element of this chakra and it is a fascinating element that connects the world of heaven and earth. Like air, our heart connects with our inner world, our emotions, and feelings along with our outer world, which we can see and touch.

Chapter 6

FIFTH CHAKRA:
THROAT OR VISHUDDHA

WILL AND EXPRESSION. MANIFEST YOUR INNER TRUTH!

TThe time has come to address the fifth chakra, which is related to the throat and responsible for the expression of your inner truth. Understand its characteristics and everything you need to know about the Vishuddha chakra in this chapter.

A good functioning of this chakra is manifested in the correct expression of your will and of your deepest desires that on some occasions, you decide to shut up out of fear or for wanting to please someone else. If you decide to act out of fear, you are betraying yourself by ignoring your deepest feelings - your real will.

Your biggest challenge is to discover what moves you to make the decisions that you make and to express what you feel whether it is your inner voice or fear speaking.

UNDERSTAND THE VISHUDDHA TO ACTIVATE ITS ENERGY

The Vishuddha chakra vibrates with an energy by which the feelings of the heart can be given voice, expressing love, forgiveness, and kindness; also, the most uncomfortable feelings such as sadness, discomfort or frustrations. Understanding the energetic consequences of your thoughts, beliefs and actions helps you to be honest with yourself and to free yourself from energetic blockages that can have unwanted manifestations in your physical or emotional body.

This fifth chakra is the center of karma, that is, of the choices and their consequences, since if you do not express your truth and decide not to listen to it, the consequences will be that you do not vibrate in tune with your inner truth and this will end up damaging you.

Its name in Sanskrit, Vishuddha, means purify; since with the energy of this chakra, it is that you release your truth to the world, you purify yourself.

It is located in the throat area and the color that represents it is blue. Those who show the most development of this energy center are people active in the use of their voice, as in the case of singers or speakers.

WHY IS THIS CHAKRA BLOCKED?

This Chakra is blocked for various reasons, the main one being when in certain situations, you refuse to verbalize your own feelings and your emotions, your inner truth that echoes your pure will and never echoes fear. When you stop yourself from manifesting your personal power to create and to communicate, you end up damaging the energy of this chakra.

Be careful with lying, because it is another significant factor that blocks the throat chakra. When you ignore your desire to express your creativity, your truth or your will and put aside your aspirations you are directly affecting this energy.

CHECKING YOUR CHAKRA

Mark the thermometer of the fifth chakra to know how your energy is at this moment. For each symptom, color in a level.

The emotional symptoms that indicate that you have a blocked Vishuddha chakra are:

- Tendency to lie and exaggerate.
- You manipulate using your words.
- Inability to speak your truth without fear.
- Bad communication in your relationships.
- Poor receptivity to the ideas of others.
- There is no coherence between your actions, wishes and words.

Physical symptoms include the following:

- Swollen lymph nodes in the neck.
- Problems with the throat or vocal cords.
- Problem with the thyroid or windpipe.
- Ear infections.

Barely living. Resurrection cart!

Struggling, hands on

Sort of surviving

Ok but some work needed

Thriving, ready for next level!

NOW START HEALING
YOUR **THROAT CHAKRA**

Express your own inner truth
and know where you stand

I SPEAK. HEAL YOUR THROAT CHAKRA!

- **Surround yourself with blue:** Blue is the color of this chakra. Stare at the blue sky and let yourself be carried away by its immensity. Dress in blue or paint a wall in this color.
- **Stones:** Use blue aventurine, blue calcite, azurite, or lapis lazuli. You can use these beautiful stones as you like. I like to wear them in some personal jewel.
- **Yoga:** Do the yoga asanas daily to activate the energy of this chakra detailed on page 81.
- **Outdoor Activities:** Sing! Choose a song that reflects what you feel, that is in tune with your "inner self", play it at full volume and indulge in the music! Nobody wants to win the next singing contest; you just want to activate the energy and have a good time. You can sing in the shower, while you walk, or while doing housework. Just enjoy the moment and surrender to your voice!

  There are times when it is impossible for us to express what we feel about something. In those cases, another way that I really like to release the trapped energy of the fifth chakra is by writing my feelings in a personal journal, making a letter to that person and letting my feelings flow freely without fear.

- **Aromatherapy:** Smell essence of eucalyptus, sage, and mint.
- **Meditation:** Do the throat chakra meditation on page 80 daily and release your chakra energy.
- **Food:** Eat nuts or seeds.
- **Mantras:** Listen and repeat the mantra HUM (hummmmm) daily.
- **Music:** Listen to the 741 Hz Frequency and leave it on.
- **Daily affirmations:** Repeat the following affirmations every day when you wake up and before going to bed:

1. I use my words to create beauty in this world.
2. I express myself easily and eloquently.
3. I express my essence in every moment.
4. I set limits clearly.

I SPEAK. HEAL YOUR THROAT CHAKRA!

Blue

Affirmations (page 78)

Blue aventurine, blue calcite or azurite

Frequency 741Hz

Asanas (page 81)

Mantra HUM

Sing or write your feelings

Eat nuts and seeds

Meditation (page 80)

Eucalyptus, sage or mint

THROAT CHAKRA MEDITATION

Do this meditation every day to balance the energy of your throat chakra:

- Sit in a comfortable position. Close your eyes.
- With each breath, draw the air through your nostrils, into your throat and lungs. Observe how it flows slowly and how it passes through your throat.
- Exhale through your mouth as if you were a dragon that shoots fire. Listen to the sound of the air leaving the body, trying to listen to the "hum" that is associated with the sound of the air leaving your body.
- Repeat listening to the sound of air going in and out.
- Repeat this chant from the ancient Sanskrit and enjoy the clear and uninterrupted sound of your voice every time the air enters and leaves your body.

Do this exercise for 3-5 minutes every day.

THROAT CHAKRA

YOGA ASANAS

Here are some postures that you can practice to open and energize your throat chakra. Stay in each pose for 3-4 minutes and breathe deeply.

MATSYASANA
FISH POSE

SIMHASANA
LION POSE

MUKHA SVANASANA
UPWARD FACING DOG POSE

SANGARVASANA
SHOULDER STAND POSE

ACTIVITIES

By freely and fearlessly expressing your emotions, and your deepest feelings, you help the energy of this chakra flow and give it more power. Just find the best way to express what you feel: Sing, write or say it out loud, whatever suits you best.

intuition
foresight
vision
perception
wisdom
psychic
illumination

--- Chapter 7 ---

SIXTH CHAKRA:
THIRD EYE OR AJNA

INTUITION AND PERCEPTION. KNOW YOUR SIXTH SENSE!

At this point, we´ve reached to the sixth chakra, which connects deeply with your intuition and perception. The sixth chakra helps us activate our senses to read between lines and establishes a balance between reason and intuition.

UNDERSTAND THE AJNA TO ACTIVATE ITS ENERGY

It is the energy center that is right between the eyebrows, in the pineal gland, also known as the blue pearl. It is related to the central nervous system.

This chakra is also known as the third eye or Ajna. This chakra opens the way to spiritual connection and allows the integration and expansion of the same consciousness.

The third eye as its name implies, represents your ability to see beyond the obvious, what your eyes do not see with the naked eye and what you do not perceive with your 5 senses or with your mind. The third eye represents your intuition, your ability to sense your inner guide and hear what your ears cannot hear.

The great challenge is learning to let yourself be guided by inner guidance and differentiate between thoughts motivated by fear and those motivated by inner strength.

If you were a company, the Ajna would be the CEO, the strategist, the one who dictates the way forward, letting himself be carried away by his long-term vision. The sixth chakra uses the wisdom and strength of the other chakras to impart its vision.

Anyone who truly manages to listen to their inner wisdom has such an exact sense of "inner self" that everything that happens in the outer world cannot exercise any control over him. This vision of the self is the basis of the wisdom with which the sixth chakra vibrates.

In summary, this sixth chakra has the following characteristics:
- It is where you can achieve the integration of the rational mind with the intuition.
- Develop the sixth sense to determine in which direction to point your next steps.
- Use the energy of the other chakras to develop intuition and read between the lines.

WHY IS THIS CHAKRA BLOCKED?

Many times, everything that surrounds you and what your rational mind tells you to do, is far from what your intuition guides you to pursue, from what your heart tells

Many times, everything that surrounds you and what your rational mind tells you to do is far from what your intuition guides you to pursue, from what your heart tells you would be the right path. When you decide not to listen to these hunches and you allow yourself to be carried away only by what your rational mind tells you to do and follow, the Ajna chakra is blocked.

Healing requires teamwork of the mind and the heart, and generally, the mind is the one that should follow the guidance of the heart, not vice versa. It is just the opposite of what we are used to acting.

On the other hand, the blind illusion is another reason why the sixth chakra is blocked; when you get excessively excited without wanting to accept reality or see beyond, you cause the blockage of the sixth chakra.

The uncontrollable thirst for power is another factor causing the blockage of this chakra; if you are in a leadership position, avoid selfishness and ambition from clouding your mind and dulling the vision of the third eye.

If the Ajna chakra is open, you have a good view of everything that surrounds you and of what is happening in your intuitive being. Your intuition is activated; you develop clarity and creative imagination.

I invite you to take the test to find out how your third eye is.

CHECKING YOUR CHAKRA

You know that you have a blocked third eye chakra when you have the following manifestations. Mark the sixth chakra thermometer to see how your energy is at this moment. For each symptom, color or mark in a level.

Emotional:
- Lack of intuition or creativity. You are not able to see beyond appearances.
- You hide in illusory worlds so as not to see reality.
- Low emotional intelligence.
- Inability to self-evaluate and learn from experiences.

Physical:
- Headaches or migraines.
- Vision problems.
- Neurological disorders.
- Epilepsy.
- Learning problems.
- Problems with the nervous system.
- Insomnia or sleep disorders.

Barely living. Resurrection cart!

Struggling, hands on

Sort of surviving

Ok but some work needed

Thriving, ready for next level!

NOW START HEALING
YOUR **THIRD EYE CHAKRA**

Your heart knows the way,
run in that direction.

Rumi

I SEE. HEAL YOUR THIRD EYE!

- **Surround yourself with indigo:** You can wear indigo or dark blue garments. This color will vibrate with the energy of this chakra.
- **Stones:** Amethyst vibrates with the energy of peace and self-awareness and this helps you to be wiser and more intuitive while it provides you with the power of observation and depth. I advise you to have one with you in your meditations to obtain more clarity, perception, as well as conscious love.
- **Yoga:** Do the recommended yoga asanas daily to activate the energy of this chakra detailed on page 93.
- **Outdoor activities:** Any activity that lets your creativity flow without restrictions will activate your third eye chakra. You can paint, do a craft, dance, or play a musical instrument. Whichever activity you choose, you just must surrender to it without trying to control it; let your inner self be the one who paints, who dances or who plays the instrument and enjoy the process.
- **Aromatherapy:** Smell essence of lemongrass, jasmine or sandalwood.
- **Meditation:** Do the third eye chakra meditation on page 92 and activate your inner guidance.
- **Diet:** Eat chocolate and purple foods, such as red onions or blueberries
- **Mantras:** Listen and repeat the OM (oooohmmm) mantra daily.
- **Music:** Listen to the 852 Hz Frequency and leave it on.
- **Daily affirmations:** Repeat the following affirmations every day when you wake up and before going to bed:

1. I trust myself and my intuition.
2. I am full of wisdom.
3. I look only for the truth.
4. My inner being guides me.

I SEE. HEAL YOUR THIRD EYE!

Indigo or light blue

Affirmations (page 90)

Amethyst, lapis lazuli or azurite

Frequency 852Hz

Asanas (page 93)

OM Mantra

Let your creativity flow

Purple foods like blueberries

Meditation (page 92)

Lemongrass, jasmine or sandalwood

AJNA CHAKRA MEDITATION

Do this meditation every day to balance the energy of your Ajna chakra:
- Light a candle.
- Sit in a comfortable position, breathe deeply, release all the muscles in your body, and gaze at the candlelight for 2 minutes. See how the flame moves freely.
- Close your eyes.
- Focus on your third eye and imagine that a bright light is there and with each breath, draw the air through your nostrils, into your throat and lungs. Watch how it flows slowly. With each breath, you feel your chakra stronger.
- Still with your eyes closed, try to visualize the burning candle with your third eye.

Do this exercise for 3-5 minutes every day.

THIRD EYE CHAKRA

YOGA ASANAS

These are some postures that you can practice to open and energize your Ajna chakra. Stay in each pose for 3-4 minutes and breathe deeply.

ADHO MUKHA SVANASANA
DOWN FACING DOG POSE

BALASANA
CHILD'S POSE

PADMASANA
LOTUS POSE

UTTANASANA
FORWARD BEND POSE

ACTIVITIES

The element of the Ajna Chakra is **LIGHT**. When we follow the light that we have within and that guides us beyond rational thought, it is when we connect with ourselves. Follow your inner intuition and let your creativity flow.

Universe • Consciousness • Awareness • Wisdom • Presence • Blisss • Divine

Chapter 8
SEVENTH CHAKRA:
CROWN OR SAHASRARA

TRANSCENDENCE AND SPIRITUALITY. KNOW YOUR GREATNESS!

We have reached the seventh and last chakra or energy center, which is purely spiritual energy. It is this energy that opens us to enlightenment and completes the process of evolution, since it connects our being to the universe.

Through the seventh chakra, we are one with the universe and we align ourselves with the most sacred expression of humanity. In this chapter, you will know all the details.

UNDERSTAND THE SAHASRARA TO ACTIVATE ITS ENERGY

Also known as Sahasrara, it is the center of wisdom and spirituality. Its vibration is responsible for the aura at the top of the head. The energy of the seventh chakra invites you to generate a connection with the divine in our day to day. This longing for connection is far removed from religions. A religion is a group of people with similar beliefs powered by the energies of the first chakra, which connect with your tribe or our family.

It is the upper chakra of the seven and is located at the crown. It is the source of illumination and spiritual connection with all that is, with our higher self, with every being on the planet and with the divine energy that creates everything in the infinite universe.

When it is open you become aware that you are pure, whole and a constantly expanding consciousness. You are aware that you are part of the ocean that contains everything and that it encompasses every aspect of itself.

It is the most subtle and ethereal of the seven chakras, the Sahasrara is the close connection with the creative power and greatness of the universe, it is not merely a brain knowledge, but something more superior: of the realization at a deeper level.

Now that you know the characteristics of the seventh chakra, I will introduce you to the reasons why it is blocked, so that you can know yourself more and live a fuller life.

WHY IS THIS CHAKRA BLOCKED?

The seventh chakra can be blocked by an imbalance with your life purpose and when you get carried away by routines, forgetting your connection with your inner being. For example, when you follow the religious beliefs of your family, without questioning whether what that religion represents is in accordance with what divinity means to you, you block the energy with which this chakra vibrates.

That is why you must take care of your vision and clarity, stay in connection with your inner being and not lose sight of your life purpose, so you can take care of falling into areas that cause imbalance and that lead to a blockage that, in turn, can generates physical, mental, emotional, and spiritual consequences.

On the other hand, when the Sahasrara chakra is open, you will have more wisdom to face each day since you are able to find yourself with your inner being without being influenced by external sensations. You will be aware of your divine presence and feel that you are connected to the universe.

CHECKING YOUR CHAKRA

A blocked crown chakra, like the previous ones, affects you in every way, generates changes in behavior, physical, emotional and mental symptoms. At the level of beliefs, a blocked seventh chakra can be identified because you lose interest in the spiritual world, you become intolerant of people who express and manifest a different religion, you think that only you have the truth, and you lose respect for others. Check the thermometer to see how your chakra is going. For each symptom, color or mark a level.

Other symptoms that allow us to know if we have a blocked crown chakra are:
- Depression due to lack of meaning in life.
- Chronic exhaustion for no reason.
- Sensitivity to light, sound, and environmental factors in general.
- Inability to communicate or connect with others.
- Lack of faith, beliefs, and spirituality.
- Intolerance to new ideas.
- Recurring headaches or migraines.

Barely living. Resurrection cart!

Struggling, hands on

Sort of surviving

Ok but some work needed

Thriving, ready for next level!

NOW START HEALING
YOUR **CROWN CHAKRA**

Why do you stay in prison when the door is wide open.

Rumi

I UNDERSTAND. HEAL YOUR CROWN!

- **Surround yourself with violet:** Violet is a receptor of divine energy, which comes to your being in the form of inspiration. Dressing in violet and visualizing this color activates the energy of this chakra so that wisdom accumulates in your energy center and helps you activate the consciousness of yourself and the universe.
- **Stones:** Use crystal quartz, moonstone, or selenite. My favorite is crystal quartz as it is the ultimate healer of all stones. Its wonderful energy will not only activate your crown chakra but will activate your vital energy.
- **Yoga:** Do the recommended yoga asanas daily to activate the energy of this chakra detailed on page 105.
- **Outdoor activities:** Any activity that is contemplative, such as observing the leaves of a tree, looking at the waves of the sea, seeing how a river flows, or simply looking at the clouds in the sky, will connect you with the universe and with your divine consciousness. Just contemplate nature in silence.
- **Aromatherapy:** Smell essence of rosewood, lotus or sandalwood.
- **Meditation:** Do the crown chakra meditation on page 104 connect with the universe daily.
- **Food:** This chakra is nourished by light, air, and love
- **Mantras:** Listen and repeat daily the HA or OM mantra (haaaaaa / ooohmm).
- **Music:** Listen to the Frequency 963 Hz and leave it on.
- **Daily affirmations:** Repeat the following affirmations every day when you wake up and before going to bed:
1. I acknowledge my own truth.
2. The divine guides my steps.
3. I am part of a whole.
4. We are all one.

I UNDERSTAND. HEAL YOUR CROWN!

Violet

Affirmations (page 102)

Crystal quartz or moonstone

Frequency 963Hz

Asanas (page 105)

OM / HA Mantra

Contemplate nature

Light, love and air

Meditation (page 104)

Essence of rosewood, lotus or sandalwood

CROWN CHAKRA MEDITATION

Do this meditation every day to balance your crown chakra energy.
- Find a secluded place where no one will interrupt you and lie down with your eyes closed.
- Imagine a bright white rain that falls on you and covers your entire body.
- Visualize how each of these glowing drops infuses your body with pure energy and feels its energy.
- Breathe deeply as your body recharges itself with peace, love, and calm.
- Visualize this for 3-5 minutes and then feel this energy settle in your body.

Repeat this exercise every day.

CROWN CHAKRA

YOGA ASANAS

Here are some poses that you can practice to open and energize your crown chakra. Stay in each pose for 3-4 minutes and breathe deeply.

VRKSANA
TREE POSE

TADASANA
STANDING MOUNTAIN POSE

NAVASANA
BOAT POSE

PARVATASANA
SEATED MOUNTAIN POSE

OUTDOOR ACTIVITIES

This wonderful energy center unites us with the universe and with divine energy; this is the door to our consciousness and spirituality. My favorite activity for activating the crown chakra is silently contemplating nature. Feeling part of the wonderful creation that is the universe and feeling its magnificence. The space around us is our connection to the universe.

CONCLUSION

I am so happy to have shared all this knowledge with you; my purpose is that you can achieve its benefit on all levels: mental, emotional, spiritual, and physical. After doing the exercises that I recommend, as happened to me, you will begin to live from another place, from a place more focused on yourself and less on others. As I call it, you will start to live more from the inside out and not the other way around.

I want you to be a full, complete being, in harmony, that you connect with your higher self, with the universe and with all those around you, that you can see all your reality with spiritual eyes and move towards the fulfillment of your mission.

My wish is that you can live in coherence with your purpose, in total healing, with full management of your emotions, with the ability to love and receive love, with the willingness to continually grow.

The knowledge of your energy centers will keep you on the path to self-improvement; it will guide you towards fulfillment and integration with the whole.
I invite you to put into practice each of the tips that I have given you, watch the signs that may point to the blockage of your chakras and take action immediately with the practices to achieve balance once again.

Keeping your energy centers healthy, open, unblocked and in balance is not a one-time thing, but it is about doing it constantly.

That is why this learning that I have shared with you and that belongs to you is for life. Take advantage of it, and you will see continuous transformations constantly.

Lead your reality; transform it according to your wishes, with your power, with your potential. Help others to find this knowledge and connect with their energy centers, thus you will be contributing to a better world, to a healthier society. That is why I invite you to share this book, recommend it to your friends, family, and acquaintances.

In the same way, go back to each chapter whenever you think it is necessary. As I have already said, keeping your chakras balanced is a daily job; so eventually, you will need to refresh your knowledge. I wish you the best experiences on this new energetic and spiritual path. It will open new horizons for you, and you will begin to see life in other colors. Welcome to your new reality!

Receive a hug. I hope we meet again in other readings.
Barbara P.E.

Made in the USA
Monee, IL
12 January 2025

76595616R00063